# THE SHOFAR

## *ANCIENT SOUNDS*
## *OF THE MESSIAH*

## Dr. Richard Booker

**The Shofar**

*Ancient Sounds of the Messiah*

Printed in the United States of America

ISBN-13: 978-0-9615302-1-1

# Table of Contents

# Preface

In the fourth century, a man named John Chrysostom (344 A.D.-407 A.D.) was the bishop of the Church of Antioch. He was a great orator. In fact, his name means "Golden-Mouthed." He had tremendous influence and is considered one of the greatest of the early church Fathers. But John Chrysostom had a problem - He hated Jews. He blamed the entire Jewish race for the death of Jesus and sought to separate Christianity from its Jewish roots.

John Chrysostom gave a series of eight sermons in which he spoke violently against the Jews. His sermons were put in written form and widely circulated. Although many early church Fathers spoke harshly against the Jews, John Chrysostom was the most vicious. His sermons fanned the flames of anti-Semitism that became the official teaching and practice of the church for the next 1,600 years.

The *Jewish-Christian Relations Series* was written to refute and rebuke the writings of John Chrysostom. It was written to express love to the Jewish people, to call the church to repentance for its anti-Semitic past and to help the church understand God's eternal purposes for the Jewish people and the nation of Israel.

The sermons given by John Chrysostom began a legacy of hate towards the Jewish people that is still with us today. *The Jewish-Christian Relations Series* was written with the hope that it will cause a new beginning of love and understanding between Christians and Jews.

# The Shofar
## Ancient Sounds of the Messiah

In 1979, I formally left my career to teach the Bible and write Christian books. My wife, Peggy, and I learned that we should incorporate our ministry. We were required to submit a name for the ministry to the proper state authorities.

Because we were still young in our walk with God, we didn't realize the power and significance of names. We considered this to be a legal process of little spiritual consequence. So without giving it much thought or prayer, we submitted a name to the state by which we would operate the ministry.

We were surprised when our application was returned because another ministry was already using the name we had selected. This got our attention. We began to ask God what name He wanted for our ministry.

During this time of seeking God's will, I was directed to the words of the prophet Joel who declared, *"Blow the trumpet in Zion, and sound an alarm in My holy mountain! Let all the inhabitants of the land tremble; for the day of the LORD is coming, for it is at hand" (Joel 2:1).*

While I was meditating on this Scripture, Peggy kept hearing in her mind the phrase, "trumpet sounding." When we connected Joel 2:1 with Peggy's thoughts, we came to believe we were to name our ministry, Sounds of the Trumpet.

From that time until now, we have both felt a strong spiritual connection to the shofar and how the Almighty used it in biblical times. For this reason, I feel compelled to share this writing on the shofar. I pray it will enlighten your mind, renew your spirit, and deepen your walk with God.

You see, in ancient times, the God of Abraham, Isaac, and Jacob used trumpets as one of His ways to communicate His instructions to His chosen people. Through the blowing of trumpets, the Lord could signal His people, prepare them for war, and call them to worship.

There were two different kinds of trumpets. In the book of Numbers we learn that the Lord commanded the people to make silver trumpets which the priests blew to:

1. call the congregation
2. direct the movement of the camp
3. sound the alarm for battle
4. call to worship for the feasts
5. announce the beginning of the new moon (month).

The text reads:

*"And the LORD spoke to Moses, saying: "Make two silver trumpets for yourself; you shall make them of*

*hammered work; you shall use them for calling the congregation and for directing the movement of the camps.*

*"When they blow both of them, all the congregation shall gather before you at the door of the tabernacle of meeting. But if they blow only one, then the leaders, the heads of the divisions of Israel, shall gather to you.*

*"When you sound the advance, the camps that lie on the east side shall then begin their journey. When you sound the advance the second time, then the camps that lie on the south side shall begin their journey; they shall sound the call for them to begin their journeys.*

*"And when the assembly is to be gathered together, you shall blow, but not sound the advance. The sons of Aaron, the priests, shall blow the trumpets; and these shall be to you as an ordinance forever throughout your generations.*

*"When you go to war in your land against the enemy who oppresses you, then you shall sound an alarm with the trumpets, and you will be remembered before the LORD your God, and you will be saved from your enemies.*

*"Also in the days of your gladness, in your appointed feasts, and at the beginning of your months, you shall blow the trumpets over your burnt offerings and over the* **sacrifices of your peace offerings; and they shall be a**

*memorial for you before your God: I am the LORD your God" " (Numbers 10:1-10).*

## The Shofar

Another type of trumpet, or horn, was the shofar. This became the most important trumpet which the Lord used to communicate with His ancient people. It is mentioned 69 times in the Hebrew Bible.

According to the *Encyclopedia Judaica*, the word shofar is related to the word *sapparu*, which means wild sheep.[1]

The shofar was made from the horn of a ram, although the horn from other kosher animals such as goats, antelopes, and gazelles could be used.

The ram's horn was primarily used because it was a ram that the Lord provided for Abraham as a sacrifice in place of Isaac, as we learn in Genesis 22.

*"Then Abraham lifted his eyes and looked, and there behind him was a ram caught in a thicket by its horns. So Abraham went and took the ram, and offered it up for a burnt offering instead of his son" (Genesis 22:13).*

When the priests blew the shofar, the people would be reminded of the mercy of the Lord in providing the ram in place of Isaac.

An interesting tradition says that the Lord preserved the two horns from the sacrificial ram given in place of Isaac. He sounded one horn at Sinai and will sound the other horn when He redeems His people by the coming of Messiah at the end of the age.[2]

The New Testament was written by Jews who also wrote that the coming of Messiah at the end of the age would be accompanied by the blowing of the heavenly shofar (1 Thessalonians 4:16; Revelation 11:15).

The people could not use the horns of cows because they were associated with the time when the Hebrews worshipped the Golden Calf as recorded in Exodus 32.

*"Now when the people saw that Moses delayed coming down from the mountain, the people gathered together to Aaron, and said to him, "Come make us gods that shall go before us; for as for this Moses, the man who brought us out of the land of Egypt, we do not know what has become of him."*

*"And Aaron said to them, "Break off the golden earrings which are in the ears of your wives, your sons, and your daughters, and bring them to me." So all the people broke off the golden earrings which were in their ears, and brought them to Aaron.*

*"And he received the gold from their hand, and he fashioned it with an engraving tool, and made a molded*

*calf. Then they said, "This is your god, O Israel, that brought you out of the land of Egypt" " (Exodus 32:1-4).*

## Preparing the Shofar

Leo Trepp explains that the ram's horn is prepared for use by first carefully removing it from the animal. It is then softened by boiling it for several hours. Next, the cartilage is removed, and a hole is drilled in the end which serves as the mouthpiece.[3]

The shofar is curved or bent to show that we are to bend our will to God as His humble servants whose hearts have been softened for use by Him.

While it is permissible to make carvings in the shofar, in rabbinic tradition, it is not considered proper to add a mouthpiece from any other material nor decorate the shofar with any foreign matter.

The reason for this is that the shofar is used to communicate the word of God. Adding foreign matter to the shofar is like adding to God's word which He emphatically forbids, as we learn in Deuteronomy 4:2 which reads,

*"You shall not add to the word which I command you, nor take from it, that you may keep the commandments of the LORD your God which I command you" (Deuteronomy 4:2).*

## The Importance of the Shofar

*The Encyclopedia of Judaism* says that the ram's horn calls upon sinners to repent, awakens thoughts of God's sovereignty, justice, and redeeming power, and expresses the Jew's hope that God will before long "sound the great shofar" to herald deliverance and the ingathering of the exiles in the land of Israel.[4]

Rabbi Wayne Dosick comments that the sound of the shofar on Rosh Hashanah "serves as a warning to people to "wake up out of their lethargy," to scrutinize their deeds, to improve their conduct, it serves as a prelude to the announcement of God's judgment; and it serves as a reminder that one day, the Kingdom of God—the time of the Messiah—will be announced to the whole world."[5]

Moses Maimonides was one of the greatest of Jewish sages. He wrote of the symbolic significance of the shofar with these words,

"Awake, O you sleepers, awake from your sleep! Search your deeds and turn in repentance. O you who forget the truth in the vanities of time and go astray all the year after vanity and folly that neither profit nor save— remember your Creator! Look at your souls, and better your ways and actions. Let every one of you abandon his evil ways and his wicked thoughts and return to God so that He may have mercy upon you."[6]

Rabbi Sha'ul (Saul; i.e., Paul) wrote similar words to the believers in Ephesus who were asleep spiritually. He said,

"... *Awake, you who sleep, Arise from the dead, And Christ [Messiah] will give you light*" *(Ephesians 5:14).*

The shofar was so important, the Bible says that the Lord Himself will blow it at His coming to redeem His people. The prophet Zechariah writes,

"*Then the LORD will be seen over them, and His arrow will go forth like lightning. The Lord God will blow the trumpet, and go with whirlwinds from the south*" *(Zechariah 9:14).*

## Use of the Trumpet and Shofar

When we read all the Scripture references to the trumpet and shofar, we learn they were used to:

## 1. Call the Assembly

"*Make two silver trumpets for yourself; you shall make them of hammered work; you shall use them for calling the congregation and for directing the movement of the camps. When they blow both of them, all the congregation shall gather before you at the door of the tabernacle of meeting*" *(Numbers 10:2-3).*

## 2. Signal or Direct the People

*" ... they shall sound the call for them to begin their journeys" (Numbers 10:6).*

## 3. Sound the Alarm for Battle

*"When you go to war in your land against the enemy who oppresses you, then you shall sound an alarm with the trumpets, and you will be remembered before the LORD your God, and you will be saved from your enemies" (Numbers 10:9).*

*"It shall come to pass when they make a long blast with the ram's horn, and when you hear the sound of the trumpet, that all the people shall shout with a great shout; then the wall of the city will fall down flat. And the people shall go up every man straight before him" (Joshua 6:5).*

(See also Judges 7; Jeremiah 4:19; 1 Corinthians 14:8.)

## 4. Call the People to Worship

*"Also in the days of your gladness, in your appointed feasts, and at the beginning of your months, you shall blow the trumpets over your burnt offerings and over the sacrifices of your peace offerings; and they shall be a memorial for you before your God: I am the LORD your God" (Numbers 10:10).*

*"Shout joyfully to the LORD, all the earth; break forth in song, rejoice and sing praises. Sing to the LORD with the harp and the sound of a psalm, with trumpets and the sound of a horn; shout joyfully before the LORD your King" (Psalm 98:4-6).*

## 5. Blown in the Presence of God

*"So David and all the house of Israel brought up the ark of the LORD with shouting and with the sound of the trumpet" (2 Samuel 6:15).*

*"Benaiah and Jahaziel the priests regularly blew the trumpets before the ark of the covenant of God" (1 Chronicles 16:6).*

## 6. Coronation of Kings

*"Then Zadok the priest took a horn of oil from the tabernacle and anointed Solomon. And they blew the horn, and the people said, "Long live King Solomon" " (1 Kings 1:39).*

## 7. Call the People to Consecrate Themselves

*"Consecrate a fast, Call a sacred assembly; Gather the elders and all the inhabitants of the land into the house of the LORD your God and cry out to the Lord. Blow the trumpet in Zion, consecrate a fast, call a sacred assembly.*

*Gather the people, sanctify the congregation, assemble the elders ..." (Joel 1:14; 2:15-16).*

8. Announce the Coming of God's Judgment

*"Blow the trumpet in Zion, and sound an alarm in My holy mountain! Let all the inhabitants of the land tremble; for the day of the LORD is coming, for it is at hand" (Joel 2:1).*

(See also Revelation 8-10.)

9. Herald the Coming of the Lord

*"Then the seventh angel sounded: and there were loud voices in heaven, saying, "The kingdoms of this world have become the kingdoms of our Lord and of His Christ [Messiah], and He shall reign forever and ever" " (Revelation 11:15).*

*"For the Lord Himself will descend from heaven with a shout, with the voice of an archangel, and with the trumpet of God. And the dead in Christ [Messiah] will rise first.*

*"Then we who are alive and remain shall be caught up together with them in the clouds to meet the Lord in the air. And thus we shall always be with the Lord. Therefore comfort one another with these words" (1 Thessalonians 4:16-18).*

*"Behold, I tell you a mystery: we shall not all sleep, but we shall all be changed—in a moment, in the twinkling of an eye, at the last trumpet. For the trumpet will sound, and the dead will be raised incorruptible, and we shall be changed" (1 Corinthians 15:52).*

## The Shofar and the Messiah

While the shofar was blown for the many purposes just stated, it was also blown to point people to the Messiah. There are six important Messianic sounds of the shofar.

1. Sound of Revelation
2. Sound of Redemption
3. Sound of Release
4. Sound of Rest
5. Sound of Repentance
6. Sound of Resurrection

## 1. The Sound of Revelation

Leon Trepp mentions that the shofar symbolizes the three important sounds of revelation, redemption, and release (freedom).[7]

It is appropriate that the shofar of revelation was the first sound of the shofar recorded in the Bible. This was when the Lord made Himself known to His covenant people at Sinai.

*"Then it came to pass on the third day, in the morning, that there were thunderings and lightnings, and a thick cloud on the mountain, and the sound of the trumpet was very loud, so that all the people who were in the camp trembled.*

*"And when the blast of the trumpet sounded long and became louder and louder, Moses spoke, and God answered Him by voice" (Exodus 19:16,19).*

## 2. The Sound of Redemption

The sound of the shofar also represented redemption. According to Isaiah, God's people will hear the shofar of redemption on the day of Israel's final ingathering.

*"So it shall be in that day; the great trumpet will be blown; they will come, who are about to perish in the land of Assyria, and they who are outcasts in the land of Egypt, and shall worship the Lord in the holy mount at Jerusalem" (Isaiah 27:13).*

## 3   The Sound of Release (Freedom)

The shofar of release (freedom) was an awesome sound to announce the year of Jubilee when all debts were canceled, slaves were set free, and the land was returned to its original owners. Anyone who had lost their land, was enslaved, or a debtor would certainly welcome this sound of the shofar.

It's interesting to note that the Hebrew word, *yovel*, is translated as Jubilee in Leviticus 25 and ram's horn in Joshua 6. The ram's horn was the sound of Jubilee and release (freedom).

*"Then you shall cause the trumpet of the Jubilee to sound on the tenth day of the seventh month; on the Day of Atonement you shall make the trumpet to sound throughout all the land.*

*"And you shall consecrate the fiftieth year, and proclaim liberty throughout all the land to all its inhabitants. It shall be a Jubilee for you; and each of you shall return to his possession, and each of you shall return to his family" (Leviticus 25:9-10).*

### 4. The Sound of Rest

The shofar was also a call to rest on the Sabbath. The Sabbath was a day to rest from one's labors. It was a day to enjoy the Lord and family. One of the Ten Commandments still says, *"Remember the Sabbath day to keep it holy" (Exodus 20:8).*

In biblical times, the shofar was used to usher in the Sabbath, God's appointed day of rest. Archeologists made a fascinating discovery a few years ago at the southern end of the Western Wall. They uncovered a huge stone block with an inscription which read in Hebrew, "To the place of the trumpeting."

It appears that this stone was located as part of a platform at the southwestern corner of the Western Wall. It had fallen when Titus destroyed the Temple in the year 70 of our era. A designated priest would stand on this platform and blow the shofar on the eve of the Sabbath.

As the sound of the Sabbath rest was heard throughout the streets of Jerusalem, the people would gladly cease from their labors and rest before the Lord.

In later rabbinic Judaism, the rabbis ruled that the shofar should not be blown on the Sabbath itself as this could be interpreted as creative work.

## 5. The Sound of Repentance

After the Temple was destroyed, and the Jewish people scattered among the nations, the shofar was mainly blown at Rosh Hashanah. Rosh Hashanah is the Jewish New Year in the month of Tishri, which is September/October on the Gentile calendar. This day is also known as the Feast of Trumpets or the "Day of the Sounding of the Shofar" from Numbers 29:1.

The shofar is blown at Rosh Hashanah to prepare the people for Yom Kippur, the Great Day of Atonement which is 10 days later. Yom Kippur is the day of soul searching and repentance. It is the day of approaching the Almighty with a broken spirit and contrite heart. The shofar blown at Rosh Hashanah is the sound of repentance.

The following is one awesome prayer of repentance given during Rosh Hashanah. It is called the *Unetane Tokef* and was written by a rabbi during the eleventh century. The prayer is during the High Holy Day Musaf service.

"Let us acclaim the majestic sanctity of this day, for it is awesome and mighty. Your kingdom is triumphantly proclaimed. Your throne is established in mercy, and you occupy it in truth.

"In truth, you are judge and prosecutor, knowing motives, giving evidence, writing, sealing, counting, measuring, remembering all, even things we have forgotten. You open the book of remembrances and it speaks for itself, for every person's signature is affixed to his deeds.

" The great shofar is sounded. A muted small voice is heard. The angels too are frightened, fear and trembling seize them, and they declare: 'This is the day of judgment, of mustering the host on high!'

"In your sight not even they are exempt from judgment. And all that have come into the world pass before you as a flock of sheep. As a shepherd gathers his flock, making his sheep pass beneath his staff; even so do you make pass, count, and muster the souls of all the living.

"You determine the latter end of every creature and record their ultimate verdict. On Rosh Hashanah it is written down for them, on Yom Kippur it is sealed. How many shall leave [live] and how many shall be born, who shall live and who shall die, who shall attain his full span of life and who shall not, who shall perish by fire, and who by water, who by the sword and who by wild beasts, who by hunger and who by thirst, who by storm and who by plague, who shall have rest and who shall be restless, who shall by repose and who shall be wandering, who shall be free from sorrow and who shall be tormented, who shall be exalted and who shall be humbled, who shall be poor and who shall be rich.

"But Repentance, Prayer, and Good Deeds can avert the severity of the decree.

"For your renown is as your name; slow to anger, ready to be soothed. You do not desire the guilty of one's death, but that he turn from his way and live. You wait for him up to the very day of his death; if he returns you accept him at once. Verily you are their Creator and you know their inner drives; they are but flesh and blood.

"As to man, his origin is dust and his end is dust, at the risk of his life he earns his bread, he is like a broken vessel of clay, like withering grass, a fading flower, a passing shadow, a drifting cloud, a fleeting breath, scattering dust, a transient dream.

"But you are King, God, living and enduring!"[8]

In actual practice, the Jewish people began preparing for the Day of Atonement the month prior to Tishri. This is the month of Elul, August/September on the Gentile calendar. In certain Jewish traditions, the shofar is blown in the synagogue each morning of the 30 days of Elul plus the 10 days from Rosh Hashanah to Yom Kippur. This gives a total of 40 days of preparation as the sound of the shofar calls the people to repentance.

**Why Blow the Shofar on Rosh Hashanah?**

In her excellent work, *The Biblical Feasts*, Robin Scarlata lists the 10 reasons that Rabbi Saadiah Gaon, a ninth century scholar, gave for blowing the shofar on Rosh Hashanah.[9]

1.  Rosh Hashanah Marks the Beginning of Creation

Jewish tradition teaches that the Lord created the universe on Rosh Hashanah. He reigns over His creation as sovereign Lord and King. As trumpets are blown to celebrate the anniversary of the reign of human kings, so the shofar is blown on the anniversary day of creation to honor the King of the Universe.

*"Shout joyfully to the LORD, all the earth; break forth in song, rejoice and sing praises. Sing to the LORD with the harp and the sound of a psalm, with trumpets and the sound of a horn; shout joyfully before the LORD, the King" (Psalm 98:4-6).*

18

2.  Rosh Hashanah is the First of the Awesome Ten Days of Repentance

The shofar prepares the people to repent of their sins. It is a warning that the Day of Judgment is at hand. Those who repent will rejoice because of the mercy of God, and their names will be inscribed in the Book of Life.

*"Blow the trumpet in Zion, consecrate a fast, call a sacred assembly" (Joel 2:15).*

3.  A Reminder of the Giving of the *Torah* at Sinai

The Lord chose to reveal Himself to the descendants of Abraham by giving them the *Torah* at Sinai. With this great privilege, came great responsibility. The blowing of the shofar at Rosh Hashanah is a reminder that, when Moses read the words of the Lord to the people, they made a commitment to listen and obey.

*"Then it came to pass on the third day, in the morning, that there were thunderings and lightnings, and a thick cloud on the mountain; and the sound of the trumpet was very loud, so that all the people who were in the camp trembled.*

*"Then he [Moses] took the Book of the Covenant and read it in the hearing of the people. And they said, "All that the LORD has said we will do, and be obedient" " (Exodus 19:16; 24:7).*

4.  A Reminder of the Words of the Prophets

The shofar is a prophetic call to declare the word of the Lord and heed His words spoken through His prophets. The prophet is like a watchman. He is accountable to the Lord to speak His words while the listener is responsible to obey. The shofar was likened to the prophetic word of the Lord given by the prophet Ezekiel.

*"... When I bring the sword upon a land, and the people of the land take a man from their territory and make him their watchman, when he sees the sword coming upon the land, if he blows the trumpet and warns the people, then whoever hears the sound of the trumpet and does not take warning, if the sword comes and takes him away, his blood shall be on his own head. He heard the sound of the trumpet, but he did not take warning; his blood shall be upon himself.*

*"But if the watchman sees the sword coming and does not blow the trumpet, and the people are not warned, and the sword comes and takes any person from among them, he is taken away in his iniquity; but his blood I will require at the watchman's hand.*

*"So you [Ezekiel], son of man: I have made you a watchmen for the house of Israel; therefore you shall hear a word from My mouth and warn them for Me" (Ezekiel 33:2-7).*

5. A Reminder of the Destruction of the Temple and War

When Titus destroyed the Temple, he also destroyed the heart of biblical Judaism. The people were scattered among the nations for centuries. But their prayer has always been, "Next Year in Jerusalem." They have longed to return to their land and rebuild the Temple as a sign of the dawning of the Messianic Age. When Jews hear the shofar blown on Rosh Hashanah, it reminds them to pray for help from the Almighty to rebuild the Temple.

*"O my soul, my soul! I am pained in my very heart! My heart makes a noise in me; I cannot hold my peace, because you have heard O my soul, the sound of the trumpet, the alarm of war" (Jeremiah 4:19).*

6. A Reminder of the Binding of Isaac

As previously mentioned, the Lord told Abraham to offer Isaac as a sacrifice to prove His devotion. The part of the story that is often overlooked is that Isaac willingly laid down his life in obedience. When we hear the shofar blown on Rosh Hashanah, we are reminded that we too must willingly give our lives as a living sacrifice to the Lord.

*"Then they came to the place of which God had told him. And Abraham built an altar there and placed the wood in order; and he bound Isaac his son and laid him on the altar, upon the wood" (Genesis 22:9).*

7.  A Call to Fear the Lord

Because the Lord is the Creator-God of the universe, we His creatures are to revere Him. The blowing of the shofar on Rosh Hashanah reminds us of His greatness and our humble position before Him. It calls us to fear Him and bend our wills to His.

*"If a trumpet is blown in a city, will not the people be afraid [fear]. If there is calamity in a city, will not the LORD have done it" (Amos 3:6)?*

8.  A Reminder of the Great Day of Judgment

While the Lord is merciful, He is also just. In His own pre-ordained time, the Lord will judge the wicked and reward the righteous. When we hear the shofar blown on Rosh Hashanah, we are reminded, that at the Great Day of the Lord, we will answer to Him for the stewardship of our lives.

Judaism also teaches that when Satan hears the shofar blown on Rosh Hashanah, he becomes confused and flees as the sound of the shofar reminds him of the coming of the Messiah.

*"The great day of the LORD is near; it is near and hastens quickly ... A day of trumpet and alarm against the fortified cities and against the high towers" (Zephaniah 1:14,16).*

9. A Reminder of the Ingathering of the Jews to Israel

Before the coming of Messiah, the Lord will gather the Jewish people from the nations and bring them back to the land He promised them and their forefathers. Once they return to the land, the Lord will circumcise their hearts to prepare them to receive their Messiah, who will establish the Kingdom of David and the Kingdom of God on the earth.

The blowing of the shofar on Rosh Hashanah reminds us of this final ingathering and that Jerusalem is the ultimate destiny of the Jewish people.

*"So it shall be in that day: the great trumpet will be blown; they will come, who are about to perish in the land of Assyria, and they who are outcasts in the land of Egypt, and shall worship the LORD in the holy mount at Jerusalem" (Isaiah 27:13).*

10. A Reminder of the Revival of the Dead

While life in the hereafter was not the focus in the First Temple era, it became more important in the times between the Testaments. As the covenant people of God suffered at the hands of the pagans, they formalized their belief that the Almighty would raise the righteous to everlasting life.

The rabbis in ancient times interpreted the following verse in Isaiah as a prophecy about the resurrection.

*"All inhabitants of the world and dwellers on the earth: when he lifts up a banner on the mountains, you see it; and when he blows a trumpet, you hear it" (Isaiah 18:3).*

When the Jewish people gather at the synagogue for Rosh Hashanah services, they recite Psalm 47 seven times before blowing the shofar. This reminds them of the seven times Joshua and the Israelites circled Jericho before the walls fell down when the shofar was blown.

Psalm 47 reads,

*"Oh, clap your hands, all you peoples! Shout to God with the voice of triumph! For the LORD most high is awesome; He is a great King over all the earth. He will subdue the peoples under us, and the nations under our feet. He will choose our inheritance for us, the excellence of Jacob whom He loves.*

*"God has gone up with a shout, the LORD with the sound of a trumpet. Sing praises to God, sing praises! Sing praises to our King, sing praises! For God is the King of all the earth; sing praises with understanding.*

*"God reigns over the nations; God sits on His holy throne. The princes of the people have gathered together, The people of the God of Abraham. For the shields of the earth belong to God; He is greatly exalted."*

## 6   The Sound of Resurrection

As mentioned, the Hebrews focused on living in this world rather than contemplating life after death. However, several Scriptures in the Hebrew Testament speak of the hope of a resurrection in the end times at the coming of Messiah. Daniel was given these words of comfort.

*"And many of those who sleep in the dust of the earth shall awake, some to everlasting life, some to shame and everlasting contempt. But you [Daniel] go your way till the end; for you shall rest, and will rise to your inheritance at the end of the days" (Daniel 12:2,13).*

Job was a man who suffered much. But he spoke these words in faith:

*"For I know that my Redeemer lives, and He shall stand at last on the earth; and after my skin is destroyed, this I know, that in my flesh I shall see God" (Job 19:25-26).*

### Blowing the Shofar

While the Lord commanded the blowing of the shofar, the Scriptures don't say exactly what sound patterns to make, nor the nature of the sounds. Over time, the rabbis agreed that three different sounds should be produced and blown in a certain order.

The first sound is the *tekiah* which is a single long blast. It is blown as a continuous rising note which ends abruptly.

While opinions vary, the *tekiah* is considered by many a call to worship and praise the Lord for His mighty creative acts. Psalm 150:3 reads, *"Praise Him with the sound of the trumpet."*

The second sound is the *shevarim*. It is made with three short blasts which are blown in a wave-like sound. This haunting sound calls the human soul to cry out to the Lord with deep sighs of repentance, brokeness and humility before the Almighty.

Isaiah reads,

*"Cry aloud, spare not; lift up your voice like a trumpet; tell My people their transgression, and the house of Jacob their sins"* *(Isaiah 58:1).*

The next sound in the order of blowing the shofar is the *teruah*. It is made with nine short staccato blasts.

These powerful blasts can be a call to warfare, victory, or celebration depending on the circumstances. Psalm 47:5 says,

*"God has gone up with a shout, the LORD with the sound of a trumpet."*

The final blast is a repeat of the *tekiah* which is a call to praise God for His mercy and goodness in redemption. This final blast is a long sustained sound which is called the *tekiah gedolah*, the great *tekiah*.

On Rosh Hashanah it is traditional to blow this sequence of blasts three different times. Altogether, a total of 100 notes are sounded. The shofar is blown once at the end of Yom Kippur.

Three times: tekia, shevarim-terua, tekia
Three times: tekia, shevarim, tekia
Three times: tekia, turua, tekia

## Jesus the Sound of Revelation

From a Christian view, the New Testament sees a connection between the shofar and the Messiah.

Jesus was a *Torah*-observant Jew. He said,

*"Do not think that I came to destroy the Law or the Prophets. I did not come to destroy but to fulfill" (Matthew 5:17).*

The Hebraic meaning of the word "fulfill" is to give the true interpretation or spiritual reality of the Law and Prophets. Jesus was claiming to be the true spiritual reality of the sound of the shofar.

As the shofar was the sound of revelation when the *Torah* was given at Sinai, Jesus came as the true meaning of Sinai. Moses wrote the *Torah* on stone tablets. But in the person of Jesus, God wrapped His *Torah* in human flesh to be the perfect revelation of the unseen Creator.

John wrote the following profound words about Jesus,

*"In the beginning was the Word, and the Word was with God, and the Word was God. And the Word became flesh and dwelt among us, and we beheld His glory, the glory of the only begotten of the Father, full of grace and truth" (John 1:1,14).*

Jesus blew the sound of revelation with His own voice when He said,

*" ... He who has seen Me has seen the Father " (John 14:9).*

Paul was a *Torah*-observant Jew. He wrote that Jesus is the image of the invisible God,

*"He is the image of the invisible God, the firstborn [heir] over all creation" (Colossians 1:15).*

The writer of Hebrews says,

*"God, who at various times and in various ways spoke in time past to the fathers by the prophets, has in these last*

*days spoken to us by His Son, whom He has appointed heir of all things, through whom also he made the worlds; who being the brightness of His glory and the express image of His person ..." (Hebrews 1:1-3).*

Jesus claimed to be the perfect revelation of the unseen God of Abraham, Isaac, and Jacob (John 14:9). To those who hear his voice, Jesus is the ultimate sound of the shofar of the revelation of the one true God.

## Jesus the Sound of Redemption

To those who hear His voice, Jesus is also the sound of redemption. When Zecharias understood that his son, John the Baptist, was to be the forerunner to Jesus, he was filled with the Holy Spirit and prophesied,

*"Blessed is the Lord God of Israel, for He has visited and redeemed His people, and has raised up a horn of salvation for us in the house of His servant David. As He spoke by the mouth of His holy prophets, Who have been since the world began" (Luke 1:68-70).*

There was an elderly prophetess named Anna who sought God in the Temple day and night with fasting and prayers. When Mary and Joseph presented the baby Jesus to the Lord, Anna knew in her heart that Jesus was the Messiah.

Luke tells the story for us,

*"Now there was one, Anna, a prophetess, the daughter of Phanuel, of the tribe of Asher. She was of a great age, and had lived with a husband seven years from her virginity; and this woman was a widow of about eighty-four years, who did not depart from the temple, but served God with fastings and prayers night and day. And coming in that instant she gave thanks to the Lord, and spoke of Him to all those who looked for redemption in Jerusalem" (Luke 2: 36 -38).*

Peter writes these powerful word about Jesus,

*"knowing that you were not redeemed with corruptible things, like silver or gold, from your aimless conversation received by tradition from your fathers, but with the precious blood of Christ [Messiah], as of a lamb without blemish and without spot" (1 Peter 1:18-19).*

In the book of Revelation, Jesus opens the sealed book to the thunderous applause of heaven. John tells us,

*"And they sang a new song, saying: 'You are worthy to take the scroll, and to open its seals; for you were slain, and have redeemed us to God by Your blood out of every tribe and tongue and people and nation, and have made us kings and priests to our God; and we shall reign on the earth" (Revelation 5:9-10).*

To those who hear His voice, Jesus is the clear sound of the shofar of redemption.

## Jesus the Sound of Release

Jesus is also the shofar sound of release, or freedom. Jesus began His ministry at the synagogue in His home town by reading the very Scripture from Isaiah that spoke of Jublilee, the Year of Release.

Jesus applied the following words to Himself,

*"The Spirit of the LORD is upon Me, because He has anointed Me to preach the gospel to the poor; He has sent Me to heal the brokenhearted, to proclaim liberty to the captives and recovery of sight to the blind, to set at liberty those who are oppressed; to proclaim the acceptable year of the LORD" (Luke 4:18-19).*

Peter wrote these words about Jesus,

*"how God anointed Jesus of Nazareth with the Holy Spirit and with power, who went about doing good and healing all who were oppressed by the devil, for God was with Him" (Acts 10:38).*

Paul declared,

*"For the law of the Spirit of life in Christ [Messiah] Jesus has made me free from the law of sin and death" (Romans 8:2).*

To those who hear His voice, Jesus sets us free from the power of sin and self-destructive habits. Whom the Son sets free is free indeed. Where the Spirit of the Lord is there is liberty.

## Jesus the Sound of Rest

Jesus is also the sound of rest. He is the true goal of the Sabbath. God gave the Sabbath as a time to rest our bodies. It was a picture of the Messiah who would give a greater rest to our souls.

Jesus was presenting Himself as the true reality of the Sabbath when He said,

*"Come to Me, all you who labor and are heavy laden, and I will give you rest. Take My yoke upon you and learn from Me, for I am gentle and lowly in heart, and you will find rest for your souls. For My yoke is easy and My burden is light" (Matthew 11:28-30).*

There is a rest for those who hear the voice of Jesus. His voice is the sound of the shofar calling us to Himself as the source of spiritual renewal for our souls.

## Jesus the Sound of Repentance

Jesus is the sound of repentance. He began His ministry with these words,

*" ... I did not come to call the righteous, but sinners to repentance" (Matthew 9:13).*

*"... Repent, for the kingdom of heaven is at hand" (Matthew 4:17).*

Then Jesus opened His mouth and spoke, like the sound of the shofar, calling people to a life of kingdom living. He said:

*"Blessed are the poor in spirit,*
*for theirs is the kingdom of heaven.*
*"Blessed are those who mourn,*
*for they shall be comforted.*
*"Blessed are the meek, for they shall inherit the earth.*
*"Blessed are those who hunger and thirst for*
*righteousness for they shall be filled.*
*"Blessed are the merciful, for they shall obtain mercy.*
*"Blessed are the pure in heart, for they shall see God.*
*"Blessed are the peacemakers,*
*for they shall be called sons of God.*
*"Blessed are those who are persecuted for*
*righteousness sake, for theirs is the*
*kingdom of heaven" (Matthew 5:3-10).*

## Jesus the Sound of Resurrection

Finally, Jesus is the sound of resurrection.

Jesus had a close friend named Lazarus who lived in Bethany with his sisters, Mary and Martha. When Lazarus died, Jesus stayed in Jericho until Lazarus was dead for a full three days and three nights.

When Jesus finally did arrive four days later, Martha said to Him,

*"Lord, if you had been here, my brother would not have died" Jesus responded, "Your brother will rise again." Martha replied, "I know that he will rise again in the resurrection at the last day." Jesus explained, "I am the resurrection and the life. He who believes in Me, though he may die, he shall live" " (John 11:21-25).*

Jesus further said,

*"Most assuredly I say to you, he who hears My word and believes in Him who sent Me has everlasting life, and shall not come into judgment, but has passed from death into life. Most assuredly, I say to you, the hour is coming and now is, when the dead will hear the voice of the Son of God; and those who hear will live. ...*

*"Do not marvel at this; for the hour is coming in which all who are in the graves will hear His voice and come forth—those who have done good, to the resurrection of life, and those who have done evil, to the resurrection of condemnation" (John 5:24-29).*

Paul gives the following words of hope and comfort to believers,

*"Now this I say, brethren, that flesh and blood cannot inherit the kingdom of God; nor does corruption inherit*

incorruption. Behold, I tell you a mystery: We shall not all sleep, but we shall all be changed—in a moment, in the twinkling of an eye, at the last trumpet. For the trumpet will sound, and the dead will be raised incorruptible, and we shall be changed.

"For this corruptible must put on incorruption, and this mortal must put on immortality. So when this corruptible puts on incorruption, and this mortal puts on immortality, then shall be brought to pass the saying that is written: "Death is swallowed up in victory." "O Death, where is your sting? O Hades, where is your victory?" The sting of death is sin, and the strength of sin is the law. But thanks be to God, who gives us the victory through our Lord Jesus Christ [Messiah].

"Therefore, my beloved brethren, be steadfast, immovable, always abounding in the work of the Lord, knowing that your labor is not in vain in the Lord" (1 Corinthians 15:50-58).

"But I do not want you to be ignorant, brethren, concerning those who have fallen asleep, lest you sorrow as others who have no hope. For if we believe that Jesus died and rose again, even so God will bring with Him those who sleep in Jesus.

"For this we say to you by the word of the Lord, that we who are alive and remain until the coming of the Lord will by no means precede those who are asleep.

*"For the Lord Himself will descend from heaven with a shout, with the voice of an archangel, and the trumpet of God. And the dead in Christ [Messiah] will rise first.*

*"Then we who are alive and remain shall be caught up together with them in the clouds to meet the Lord in the air. And thus we shall always be with the Lord. Therefore, comfort one another with these words"* (1 Thessalonians 4:13-18).

## Personal Application

Clarence Wagner, former International Director of Bridges for Peace, has pointed out that for each of these uses of the shofar, we can find a personal application for our own lives.

Each of us must ask ourselves, "What sound of the shofar is God blowing for me to hear?"

Is He calling me to assemble or come before Him? Does He want to give new direction for my life? Is He calling me to spiritual warfare against the enemies of God?

Is He calling me to worship Him more intimately? To be in His presence? To crown Him King of my life? To consecrate myself to Him with a greater commitment? To judge the sin in my life? To prepare for His coming?

Does God want to reveal something to me? Is there an area of my life He wants to redeem? Is He calling me to release something that I've been holding on to? Is there a place of rest in Him that I haven't yet found? Is the sound to repent?

There's an interesting Scripture in Jeremiah that reads,

*"Also I set watchmen over you, saying, 'Listen to the sound of the trumpet!' But they said, 'We will not listen' " (Jeremiah 6:17).*

As we ponder this Scripture, let us not be like those who would not listen. Let us hear and obey the sound of the shofar the Lord is blowing for our lives.

The Lord says through the prophet Hosea, *"Set the trumpet to your mouth ..."* (Hosea 8:1).

We are all called to sound the shofar of God's love, redemption, and righteous judgment through our words and our deeds.

During Rosh Hashanah, the Jews offer the following prayer, "Blessed be Thou O Lord our God King of the universe, who has sanctified us by Thy commandments and instructed us to hear the call of the shofar."

May we hear the call of the shofar for our own lives and be a clear sound proclaiming His voice to our world.

## ENDNOTES

[1]*Encyclopedia Judaica*, (Jerusalem: Keter Publishing House, Jerusalem Ltd., 1972), Volume 14, pages 1443.

[2]Leo Trepp, *The Complete Book of Jewish Observance* (New York: Berhman House, Inc./Summit Books, 1980), 95.

[3]Ibid., 94.

[4]Geoffrey Wigoder, Editor-in-Chief, *The Encyclopedia of Judaism* (New York: Macmillan Publishing Company, 1989), 653.

[5]Wayne Dosick, *Living Judaism* (New York: HarperCollins, 1995), 133.

[6]Eckstein, Yechiel. *What Christians Should Know About Jews and Judaism* (Waco, TX: Word, Inc., 1984), 119.

[7]Trepp, 95.

[8]Eckstein, 121-122.

[9]Robin Scarlata, *The Biblical Feasts* (Madison, TN: Family Christian Press, 1996), 266.

## SCRIPTURE REFERENCES

The following Scriptures refer to the trumpet and/or shofar as listed in the Strongs Concordance.

**Trump**

1 Corinthians 15:52
1 Thessalonians 4:16

**Trumpet**

Exodus 19:13, 16, 19; 20:18
Leviticus 25:9
Numbers 10:4
Joshua 6:5, 20
Judges 3:27; 6:34; 7:16,18
1 Samuel 13:3
2 Samuel 2:28; 6:15; 15:10; 18:16; 20:1, 22
1 Kings 1:34, 39, 41
Nehemiah 4:18, 20
Job 39:24
Psalm 47:5; 81:3; 150:3
Isaiah 18:3; 27:13; 58:1
Jeremiah 4:5, 19, 21; 6:1, 17; 42:14; 51:27
Ezekiel 7:14; 33:3,4,5,6

**Trumpet (Continued)**

Hosea 5:8; 8:1
Joel 2:1, 15
Amos 2:2; 3:6
Zephaniah 1:16
Zechariah 9:14
Matthew 6:2; 24:31
1 Corinthians 14:8; 15:52
Hebrews 12:19
Revelation 1:10; 4:1; 8:13; 9:14

**Trumpeters**

2 Kings 11:14
2 Chronicles 5:13; 29:28
Revelation 18:22

**Trumpets**

Leviticus 23:24

## Trumpets (Continued)

Numbers 10:2,8,9,10; 29:1; 31:6
Joshua 6:4,6,8,9,13,16,20
Judges 7:8,18,19,20,22
2 Kings 9:13; 11:14; 12:13
1 Chronicles 13:8; 15:24, 28; 16:6, 42
2 Chronicles 5:12,13; 7:6; 13:12,14; 15:14; 20:28; 23:13;
29:26,27
Ezra 3:10
Nehemiah 12:35,41
Job 39:25
Psalm 98:6
Revelation 8:2-6

## About the Author

Dr. Richard Booker is a Bible teacher and author known for his ability to communicate difficult subjects in an easy-to-understand manner. He has written many best-selling books which have touched the lives of people around the world.

In 1974, God dramatically changed Richard's life while he was studying the book of Leviticus. He saw Jesus in every book of the Bible. Afterwards, Richard left his successful business career to teach and write about the insights God was giving him.

Richard, along with his wife, Peggy, travel extensively sharing God's Word with clarity and love to both Christians and Jews. *If you would like for Richard to come to your church, congregation, conference or study group, contact him at his office address.*

Dr. Booker has written 38 books and developed 19 college level courses on the Bible from a Judeo-Christian perspective. He has also made over 500 Christian television programs and serves as a spiritual father to many, He and Peggy have led tour groups to Israel for 25 years, where for 18 years, Dr. Booker was a featured teacher for the international Christian celebration of the Feast of Tabernacles in Jerusalem.

Richard is the founder of Sounds of the Trumpet, Inc. and the Institute for Hebraic-Christian Studies (IHCS). IHCS provides courses on the Hebraic roots of Christianity leading to a Diploma in Hebraic-Christian Studies. *See website for more information.*

Richard has an M.B.A. and a Ph. D. in Theology.

## Books on the Hebraic-Jewish Roots of Christianity
## by Dr. Booker

### *Here Comes the Bride*
One of the most beautiful pictures of God's love is the ancient Jewish wedding. This book explains Jewish wedding customs and how they point to the Messiah as well as what we can do to prepare ourselves for the greatest event of the ages, the wedding of God's bride.

### *Shabbat Shalom*
While the Sabbath is central in Jewish life, many Christians are being called by God to discover the Jewish roots of their faith. This publication explains what the Bible says about the Sabbath and how Christians can celebrate the Sabbath in their own homes.

### *How the Cross Became a Sword*
This book explains the events that separated Christianity from its Jewish roots and established anti-Semitism as official church doctrine. It then gives an excellent overview of the tragic history of Christian-Jewish relations directly linking modern replacement theology to the first Christian seminary in Alexandria, Egypt.

### *Islam, Christianity, and Israel*
This book reveals the shocking information about the life of Mohammed and the background, teachings and practices of Islam. The reader learns how Islam differs from Christianity and the truth about the conflict between the Arabs and the Jews which you won't learn from the evening news.

### The Time to Favor Zion Has Come
One of the greatest events of our times is the rebirth of the State of Israel. This book explains the prophetic aspects of the final ingathering of the Jewish people back to their land in preparation for the coming of Messiah. You will learn how the Jews are being regathered, restored, and redeemed.

### The Shofar: Ancient Sounds of the Messiah
This book explains the background, purposes, and use of the shofar in ancient and modern times and how the shofar called the people to a deeper walk with God through the Messiah.

### Blow the Trumpet in Zion
This book explains the dramatic and fascinating story of the Jewish people, Israel and the nation in prophecy. It is one of the most comprehensive books relating Bible prophecy to world history and current and future events as they revolve around God's covenant plan for Israel.

### Celebrating Jesus in the Biblical Feasts
This is a study of the Feasts of the Lord showing how they pointed to Jesus and their personal and prophetic significance for today's world. It reveals how the Feasts represents seven steps in the believer's walk with God,

### The Miracle of the Scarlet Thread
This is a worldwide best-selling classic on the blood covenant and how it pictures the Messiah in connecting the two Testaments in the Bible to tell one complete story. It is considered standard reading for believers around the world.

### No Longer Strangers

This is a comprehensive introduction to the Hebraic-Jewish roots of Christianity. The text is well-documented with footnotes, a helpful bibliography, and an index for easy reference. Dr. Booker explains Christian and Jewish history, beliefs and practices, how Christianity and Judaism relate, and much more.

### Torah: Law or Grace

This is one of the most eye-opening books you will ever read. You will discover the true meaning of law and grace, how these powerful words have been misunderstood, the prophetic restoration of their true meaning, and the significance this has for your life today.

### Ancient Jewish Prayers and the Messiah

This profound book will revolutionize your life. You will discover the Jewish background to Christian prayers, the Jewish background to the "Lord's Prayer" and the most important prayer in Judaism that concerns events regarding the restoration of Jerusalem and the coming of Messiah.

### Discovering The Miracle of the Scarlet Thread in Every Book of the Bible

This book takes the mystery out of the Bible as Dr. Booker explains the master theme of the Bible showing Jesus and the blood covenant story in every book of the Bible.

### The Root and Branches

This is an orientation course for those just beginning their study of the Jewish roots of Christianity. It is Jewish Roots 101.

*For more information on these and other life-changing books by Dr. Booker, see his website and online store at www.rbooker.com*

Made in the USA
Monee, IL
04 August 2024